Contents

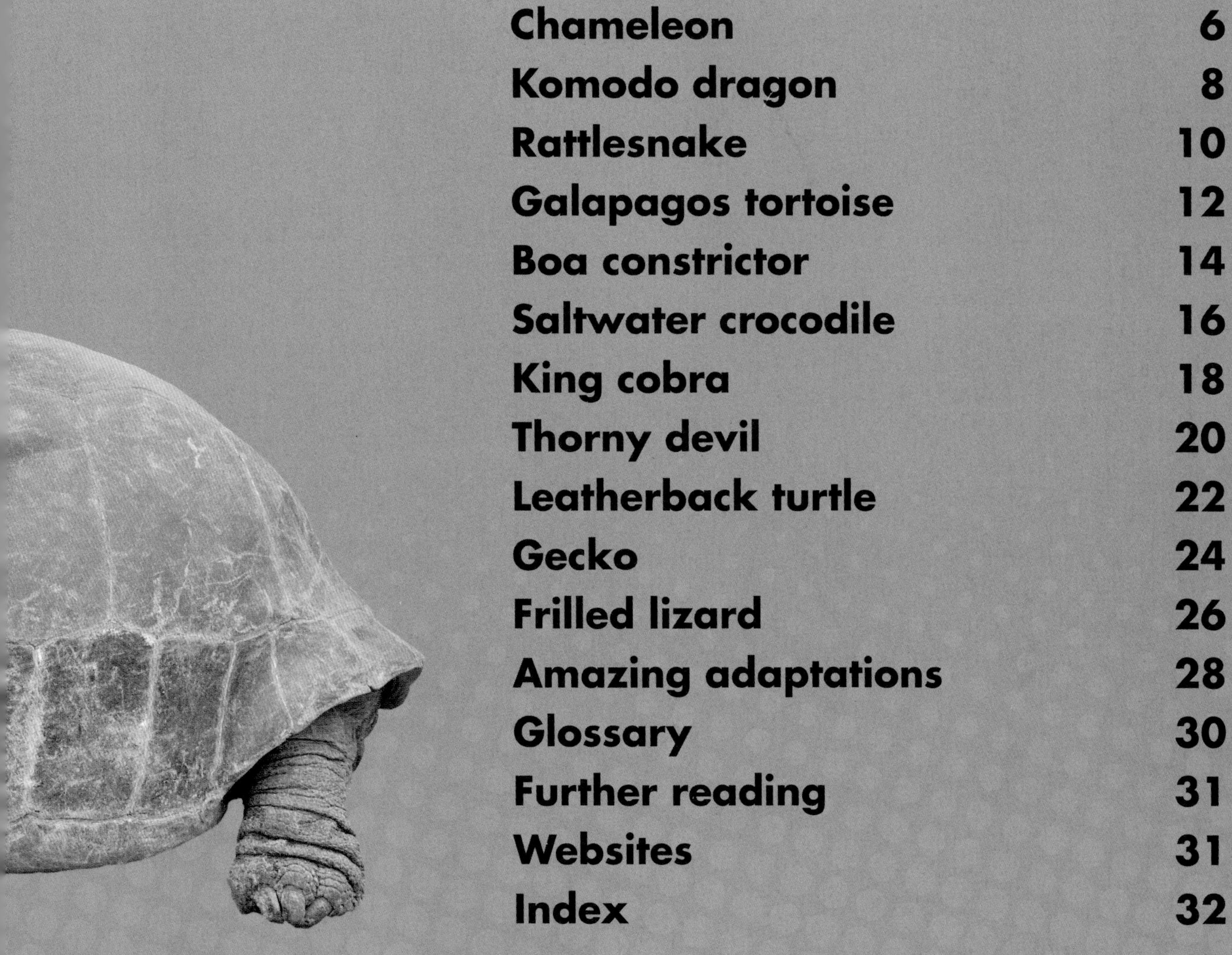

Reptiles

There are more than 6,500 different types of **reptile** in the world. They are all amazing in their own way. Reptiles come in many different shapes and sizes. Some spend most of their time in water, others live on land. Different reptiles may look and live differently, but they all have some things in common.

All reptiles are **vertebrates**. They have a backbone (spine).

All reptiles have scales or horny plates on their skin.

All reptiles are **cold-blooded**, which means they cannot control their body temperature. They must warm up in the Sun or cool down in the shade.

Reptile superstars

All reptiles are amazing, but some are more astonishing than others! In this book we are going to find out about some of the world's most talented reptile superstars.

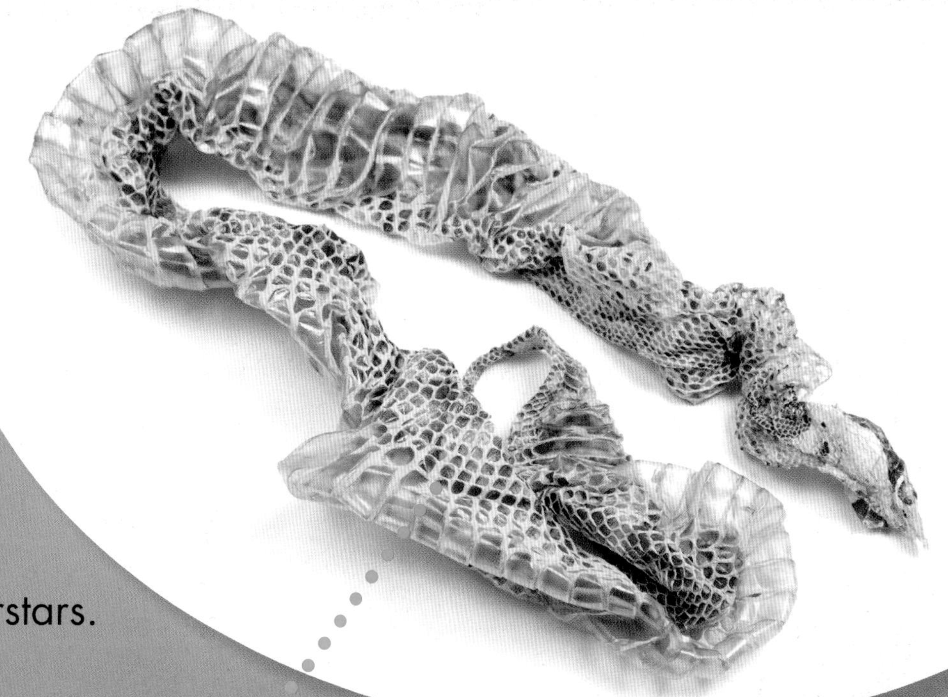

Snakes and some lizards regularly shed their entire skin as they grow bigger, and replace it with a new one beneath.

Secret stars

The tuatara looks like a lizard but it is, in fact, the only remaining species of a reptile group that lived during the time of the dinosaurs! This animal has a bizarre feature, a third eye on the top of its head. In adults, the eye is covered by **scales**, but is sensitive to light and may help tuataras tell the time or season.

Chameleon

Quick change artist

The chameleon can make the quickest costume changes you will ever see! This reptile's skin can swiftly and dramatically change colour and pattern. Chameleons change colour in response to heat or light, and to communicate with other chameleons.

When cold, the chameleon becomes darker, because dark colours absorb more heat than light colours. When a male wishes to attract a female, its colour becomes brighter.

Tongue-tastic!

Chameleons use their incredibly long tongue to catch the insects they eat. Chameleons flick out their tongues to catch insects at a rate that is too fast for the naked eye to see. The animal's tongue moves in and out 26 times per second. It is as long as the chameleon's body and can stretch more than three times its length.

The tongue has a sticky tip to trap insects before they have a chance to fly away.

The tongue pulls **prey** quickly back into the mouth, where the animal's strong jaws crush it.

Top talent

Chameleons have swivelling eyes that can look at two different things at once! One eye can point forwards to look for food, while the other can look upwards, to the side, or even directly behind to keep a lookout for **predators**.

Komodo dragon

Heaviest lizard

Make way for the heaviest lizard on Earth! This fearsome-looking heavyweight grows to a length of 3 metres and a weight of 35 kilograms. These huge creatures need to eat large amounts of food. They catch and eat prey as big as water buffalo and deer.

The Komodo dragon can eat 80 per cent of its own body weight at one time.

Killer bite

Sometimes an animal manages to wriggle free from the Komodo's killer jaws, but it does not escape. When the Komodo dragon bites, it releases **venom** into the wounds of its prey. The victim later dies, and the Komodo tracks down the body and eats it.

The Komodo dragon opens its mouth wide to deliver a deadly, poisonous bite.

Secret stars

Contenders for the smallest lizards in the world are the miniature chameleons of Madagascar. These miniscule marvels look very similar to an adult chameleon, but they are small enough to stand on the tip of a matchstick!

A Komodo dragon uses its strong leg muscles and heavy claws to attack prey.

A Komodo dragon can run short distances at speeds up to 20 km per hour (13 mph), but it prefers to wait for prey to pass rather than chase it.

Rattlesnake

Super sensors

The rattlesnake hunts at night. It has superb senses that help it track down prey, even in complete darkness. The snake has small heat-sensing pits on each side of its head. The pits tell the snake where small mammals, such as rodents, are by sensing their body heat. The rattlesnake then closes in and strikes!

The rattlesnake can grow up to 2.5 metres long.

Rousing rattles

The rattlesnake is named after the rattle at the end of its tail. This is made up of rings of keratin, which is the same material found in fingernails. When a predator approaches, the snake puffs up its body and shakes its tail. When the rings of keratin rattle together, they make a frightening hissing sound that scares off many predators!

Top talent

Small mammals are not safe from the rattlenake even in water, because the snake is an excellent swimmer. It takes to water to chase prey, follow mates and to escape predators or people. Some rattlesnakes have been seen several kilometres out at sea.

Galapagos tortoise

Oldest vertebrate

Most Galapagos tortoises live for about 100 years and some even live to the grand old age of 150! Not only are these gentle giants one of the world's oldest living vertebrates, they are also the largest tortoises on Earth. Some are more than 1.5 metres long and 250 kilograms in weight.

The tortoise saves energy by napping in the Sun for almost 16 hours a day!

The tortoise's tough shell is surprisingly light because it is filled with hollow spaces.

The tortoise has sturdy legs to hold up the heavy weight of its giant body.

Secret stars

Like Galapagos tortoises, Galapagos marine iguanas are found only on the Galapagos Islands off South America. These amazing animals scrape seaweed from rocks to eat. They sneeze regularly, to get rid of salt from the seawater they swallow. The salty waste often lands on the animals' heads, giving them a strange white patch on their forehead.

Slow and steady!

A Galapagos tortoise feeds lazily on grass, leaves and cactus fruit. It has no teeth, but its heavy beak has sharp edges that tear and bite through tough plants. This sleepy creature can last for a year without food or drink. It survives by using little energy and breaking down its body fat to make water.

Boa constrictor

Tightest hug

This enormous snake gives the tightest hug. The embrace is not a sign of affection, however, but a means by which to catch dinner! The snake lies in wait for an animal to pass. Then it darts out, grabs the prey and coils its body around it. The snake then squeezes its prey to death.

A boa constructor has 400 ribs in its backbone so it can wrap its body around its prey many times.

The boa grows up to 4 metres long. It can easily catch and eat big animals such as wild pigs.

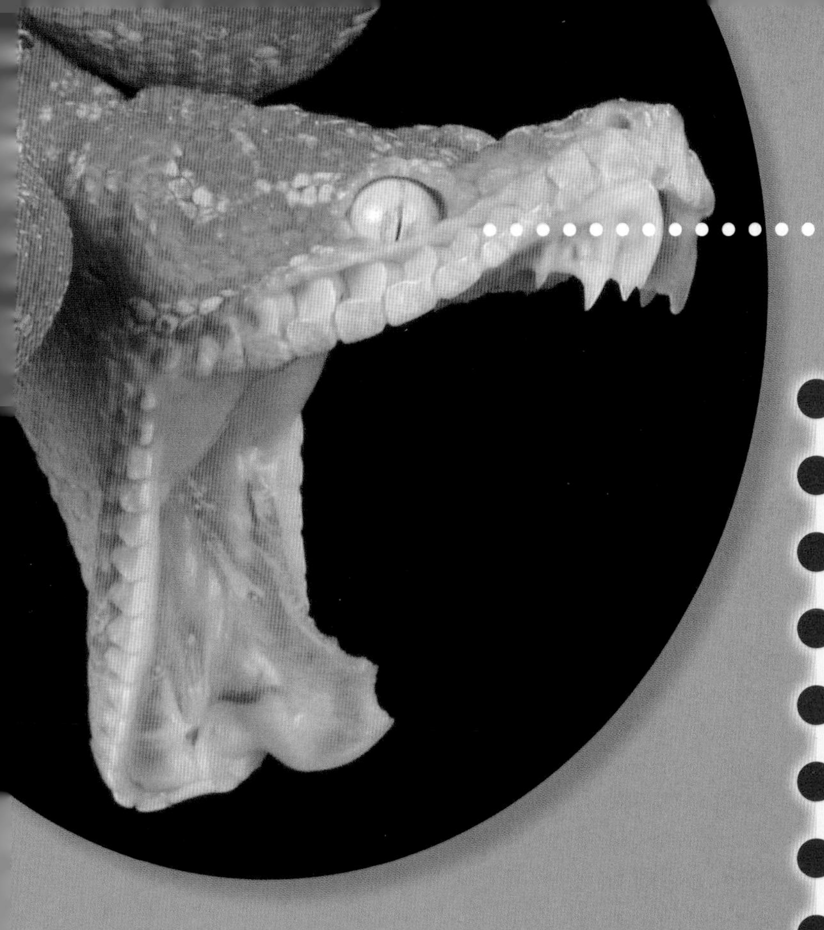

A boa's jaws unhinge so it can open its mouth wide and swallow prey whole.

Open wide!

A boa constrictor can swallow even big animals whole. The **ligaments** that connect the bones in the snake's jaws are flexible, allowing it to open its mouth wide. The snake swallows prey headfirst. Then, muscles inside its body squeeze the prey down through the throat and into the stomach. After a large meal, boa constrictors may not need to eat again for several weeks.

Top talent

Even tree-living animals cannot escape the boa's clutches. The snake's tail is partly prehensile. That means it can grasp and hold. The boa climbs trees by wrapping its tail tightly around a branch or trunk for support. The snake's colors also **camouflage** it against trees, helping it hide from prey.

Saltwater crocodile

World's largest reptile

The awesome saltwater crocodile is huge. Some adult males grow to be 7 metres long. That is longer than four adult men lying head to toe! These terrifying, toothy giants eat almost anything they can fit in their huge mouths, from monkeys to water buffaloes.

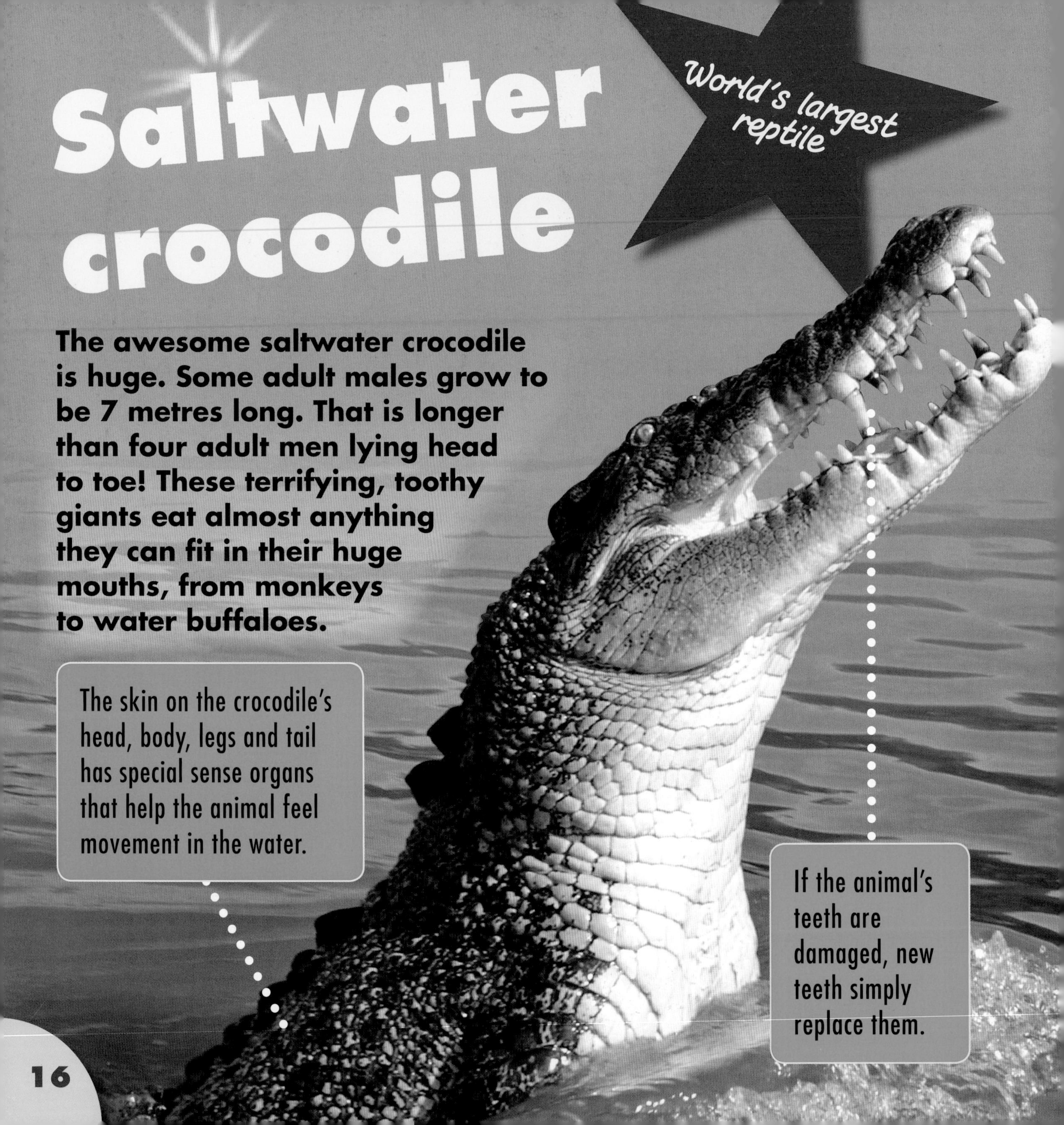

The skin on the crocodile's head, body, legs and tail has special sense organs that help the animal feel movement in the water.

If the animal's teeth are damaged, new teeth simply replace them.

Log lookalike

A crocodile can lie just beneath the water so it looks like a floating log. It can hold its breath for more than an hour! When unsuspecting animals come to the water's edge to drink, the crocodile shoots out of the water, grabs its victims in its teeth, and drags them into a watery grave.

The crocodile's eyes are on top of its head so it can still see all around when in the water.

Baby crocodile

Top talent

Crocodiles are one of the few reptiles that protect their young until they are old enough to live on their own. Females bury their eggs in a nest of mud and plants, and guard the eggs until they hatch three months later. Then, these perfect mums carry their babies gently between their teeth to the water, and care for them until they can swim.

King cobra

Scariest snake

The king cobra is one of the world's most dangerous and frightening snakes. When it is angry or scared, it lifts the front part of its body off the ground, spreads its hood and hisses fiercely. The sound is terrifying! From this position, the majestic king cobra is ready to strike.

The hood around the cobra's neck is loose so the snake can spread it out to make itself look bigger and scarier.

When raised up off the ground, the snake is tall enough to see eye to eye with an adult man!

The king cobra can grow up to 5.6 metres long and is the world's longest venomous snake.

Deadly bite

When the king cobra hunts snakes and lizards, it lunges forward in a swift and deadly attack. It thrusts its sharp, hollow fangs into prey and injects a poison that kills them quickly. In fact, the amount of venom in just one cobra bite is enough to kill an adult elephant or even 20 people!

Some cobras can even spit their venom at victims, too.

Top talent

The Indian cobra has another secret skill. When it spreads its hood, it reveals false eyespots on the back of the hood. These circular patterns and lines look like eyes and the snake uses them to scare away any predators that approach it from behind.

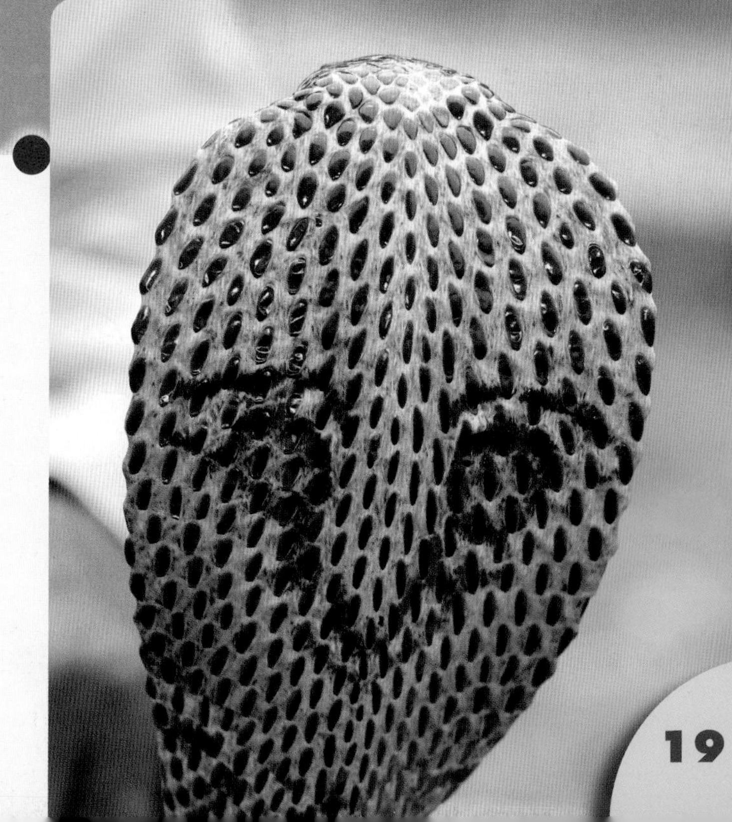

Thorny devil

Sharpest spines

The thorny devil is a sinister-looking lizard that has large, sharp spines all over its body and tail. This coat of spikes makes the lizard fearsome, but it is, in fact, harmless. The spikes protect the lizard from predators while it quietly goes about its business, munching up to 5,000 ants in a single meal!

Cone-shaped, sharp spines stop most predators biting or swallowing the thorny devil.

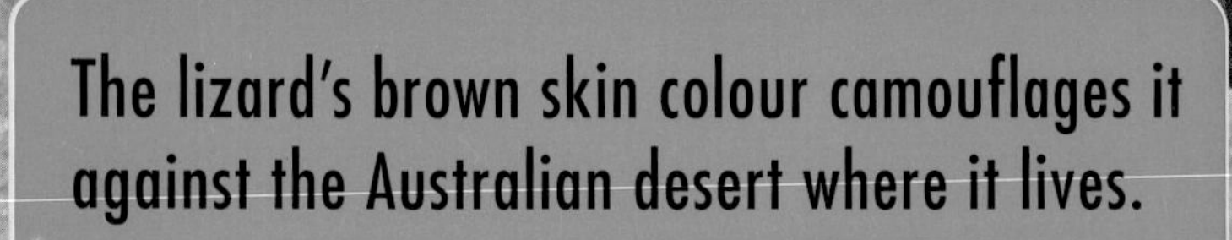

The lizard's brown skin colour camouflages it against the Australian desert where it lives.

Thirsty work

Its spikes also stop the thorny devil from becoming too thirsty in the dry desert where it lives. Between the lizard's scales are grooves within which droplets of morning dew and water from damp desert sand collect. The spines are shaped to ensure the collected water flows into the lizard's mouth.

The thorny devil can collect water from any part of its spiny body.

Secret stars

Horned toads are lizards that are named after their flat toad-like bodies. Like the thorny devil, these lizards have spikes all over their body, but they have other defences, too. They swallow air to inflate their bodies to make them seem bigger. They can also spurt blood from their eyes.

Leatherback turtle

Deepest diver

This 2 metre-long sea turtle takes the gold medal for being the deepest reptile diver. When the turtle swims into deep water to catch its prey, it can reach depths of 1,200 metres. That is almost as deep as three New York Empire State Buildings!

The turtle does not have a hard shell. It is named after the thin, leathery, flexible skin that covers its back.

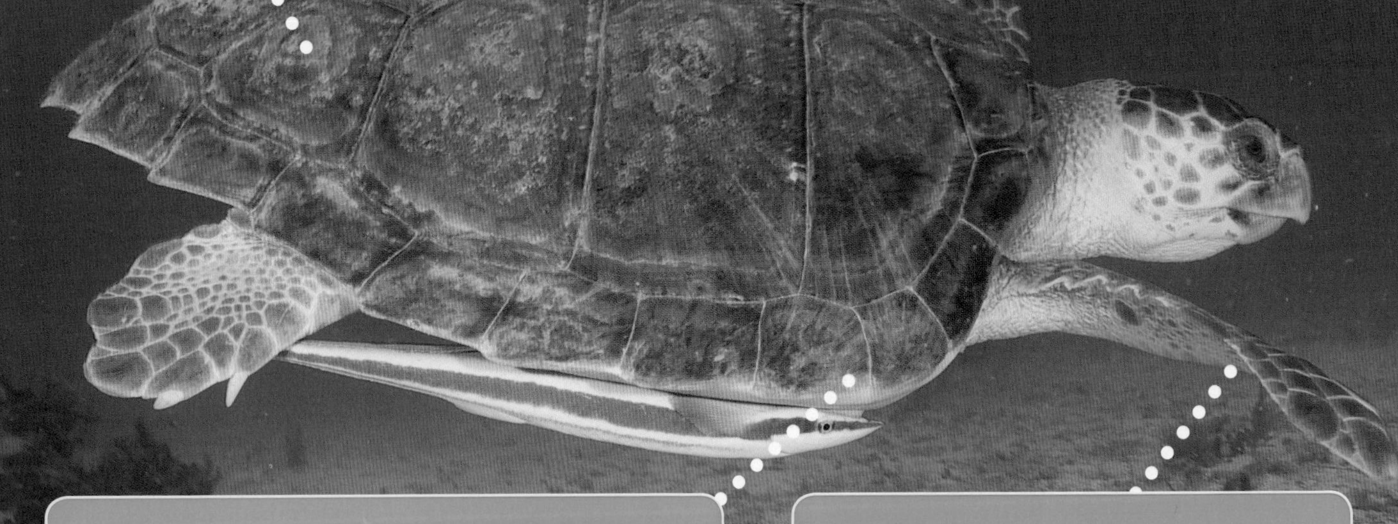

The leatherback turtle can hold its breath for 30 minutes before coming up for air.

The turtle's front flippers can be up to 3 metres long. They help it swim in deep water.

Sadly, some leatherbacks die when they swallow plastic bags that they mistake for jellyfish.

Dinner time

Leatherback sea turtles dive deep to feed on jellyfish and squid. The leatherback turtle has backward-curving spikes in its mouth and throat. Once the turtle catches a jellyfish, the animal becomes hooked on the turtle's spikes and cannot free itself.

Top talent

Leatherbacks have paddle-shaped back **flippers** that help them swim long distances. The turtles swim about 7,000 km (4,350 miles) across oceans, from waters where they feed to beaches where they lay eggs.

Gecko

The gecko is a world-class climber. This cute, lively lizard can scale a sheer, smooth rock face in minutes to chase after the flies it eats. The gecko is also a show-off! It can hang from a ceiling using just one toe, and can even cling to a glass window. In fact, the gecko is the Spiderman of the animal kingdom!

If a predator catches it by its tail, the gecko simply loses its tail to escape and grows a new one.

Geckos do not have eyelids so they cannot blink. Instead, they have a clear layer of tissue to protect their eyes from dirt and harsh sunlight.

Hairy toes

The secret to the gecko's super climbing skills is its hairy toes. Each toe on the gecko's foot is covered with clumps of tiny hairs. The end of each hair is shaped like a sucker. The gecko rolls these hairs onto the surface, and then peels them off again, just like peeling sticky tape.

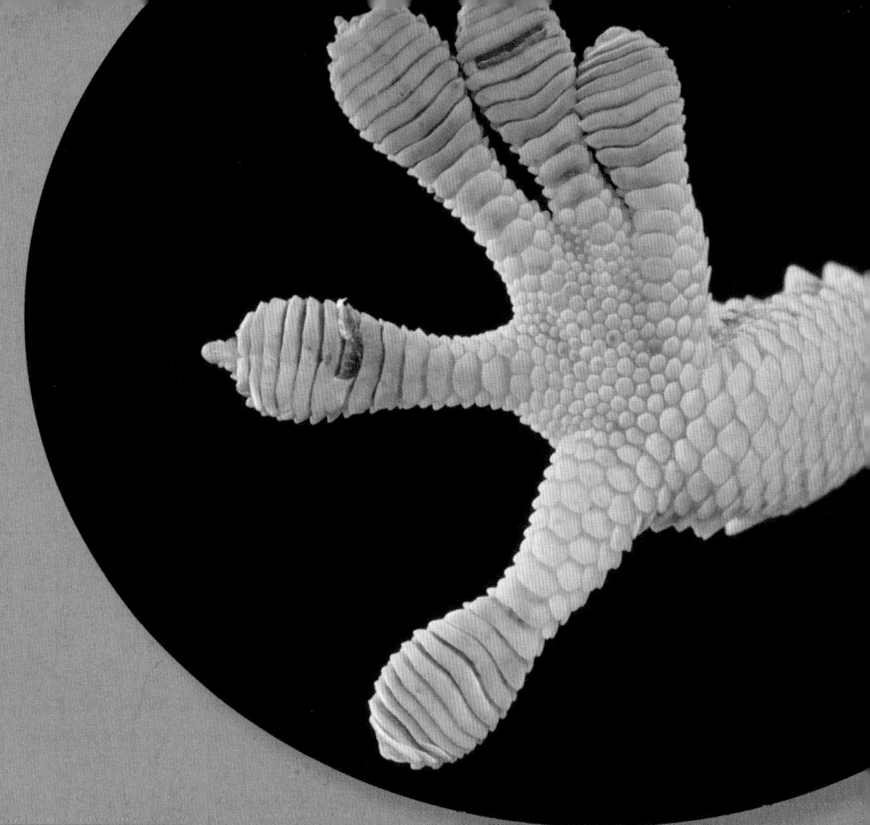

Secret stars

The gecko might be able to run up smooth walls, but the green crested basilisk is a lizard that can run on water! When the basilisk is scared, it sprints so speedily on its back legs that it can run across the surface of a pond for over a metre before diving underwater.

Frilled lizard

Funniest display

Frilled lizards are one of Australia's strangest-looking lizards. This comical clown has a frill of loose, pleated skin that usually hangs around its neck like a cape. When the lizard is frightened, it opens out the frill, like an umbrella. This makes the lizard appear much bigger and scarier than it really is.

The frill on the frilled lizard can measure up to 30 cm wide.

The frilled lizard also opens its brightly coloured mouth wide and hisses at predators or rival lizards.

Crafty dodger

If a predator approaches the frilled lizard when in a tree, the lizard moves to the opposite side of the tree trunk. If the predator walks around the bottom of the tree, the lizard dodges around the trunk to stay out of sight!

Secret stars

The anole has a way of showing other males how fit and strong it is. Every morning and evening, the lizard performs a workout that includes energetic push-ups, head bobs and the unfurling of the colourful flaps beneath its chin!

If its huge frill and hissing mouth does not scare away its enemy, the frilled lizard prances away quickly on its back legs!

Amazing adaptations

Animals develop special body features to help them survive. These are called **adaptations.** Physical adaptations are features such as the hard shell of a tortoise or turtle, which protects the animals from predators. The harmless Sinaloan milk snake has red and yellow rings to make it look like the poisonous coral snake, to stop birds from attacking it.

The fringe-toed lizard has a fringe of special scales on its back toes to help it grip the sand as it runs across dunes.

The sidewinder is the fastest of all rattlesnakes because of its special way of moving.

Behavioural adaptations

Some adaptations are behavioural. These are things that animals do to survive. For example, a sidewinder snake moves swiftly across deserts in a sideways, S-shaped pattern so that its body barely touches the burning hot sand. Many reptiles that live in the desert are **nocturnal**. They come out only at night to avoid the heat of the day.

Top talent

The scales on the skins of reptiles allow these animals to live all over the world, except in the ice-cold tundra. Scales are tough enough to protect the reptile's insides and hold water in their bodies to stop them from drying out in very hot places. Scales range from the hard scales of a crocodile to the soft, smooth scales of a corn snake.

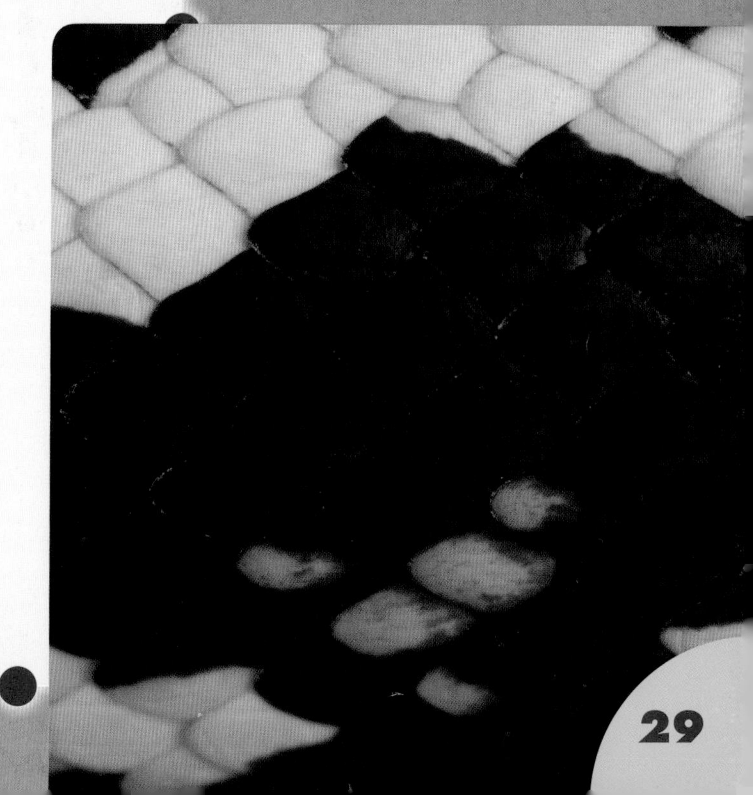

Glossary

adaptations features or ways of behaving that help animals survive

camouflage natural colouring or shape of an animal that allows it to blend in with its surroundings

cold-blooded system in which the body temperature of an animal stays close to that of its surroundings

fangs large, very sharp teeth

flippers limbs on the body of a marine animal, such as a turtle. Flippers are used for swimming.

ligaments flexible body parts that hold an animal's bones together

mammals animals that have live young and feed their offspring with milk from their body

nocturnal sleep during the day and be active during the night

predators animals that hunt and eat other animals

prey animal that is hunted and eaten by other animals

reptile cold-blooded, air-breathing vertebrate that usually lays eggs and has skin covered with scales or bony plates

scales small stiff, flat plates that overlap to form an outer covering on a reptile's body

venom poison

vertebrate animal with a backbone

Further reading

Reptile: Discover The Intriguing World of Reptiles (Eyewitness), Various authors (DK Children, 2017)

Reptiles (Focus On), Stephen Savage (Wayland, 2015)

Why Do Reptiles Have Gills? (Wildlife Wonders), Pat Jacobs (Franklin Watts, 2016)

Websites

www.bbc.co.uk/guides/zp9pfg8
Test your knowledge of reptiles in this fun quiz!

www.dkfindout.com/uk/animals-and-nature/reptiles/
Find out more about reptiles' behaviours and features, plus more astounding reptile facts and photographs.

Index